SAYING HELLO
AT THE STATION

Selima Hill

CHATTO & WINDUS

THE HOGARTH PRESS

LONDON

Published in 1984 by
Chatto & Windus · The Hogarth Press
40 William IV Street
London WC2N 4DF

British Library
Cataloguing in Publication Data

Hill, Selima
Saying hello at the station.
I. Title
821′.914   P160581/

ISBN 0-7011-2788-0

Phototypeset by Rowland Phototypesetting Ltd
Bury St Edmunds, Suffolk
Printed in Great Britain by
Redwood Burn Ltd
Trowbridge,
Wiltshire

Contents

Acknowledgements

Acknowledgements are due to the editors of the following magazines in which some of these poems first appeared:
The London Review of Books; Poetry Review; Writing Women.

'Chicken Feathers' was one of the prize-winning poems in the Sotheby's/ Arvon Poetry Competition 1982.

In the Flaubert poems, I am indebted to the letters and notebooks which he wrote during his visit to North Africa with Maxime du Camp in 1849, the year before he began *Madame Bovary*.

In 'Above Tooey Mountain', I am indebted to the letters of Sir James Melville, James Joyce's mother, and Gerard Manley Hopkins (written on the day that he died).

A dream-hole is an architectural term for a hole left in the walls of towers and steeples to admit light.

In climes beyond the solar road
   Where shaggy forms o'er ice-built mountains roam,
The Muse has broke the twilight gloom,
   To cheer the shivering native's dull abode.

     from *The Progress of Poesy* by Thomas Gray

Questioning Mr Bonnet

Mr Bonnet, the helpful Egyptologist,
explains the strange cosmology
in his Reallexikon der ägypschen
Religionsgeschichte that he wrote
when he was dying in Berlin:
Horus, the god of light, hid his semen
in a dish of chopped lettuce leaves,
and greedy Seth, the god of darkness,
pig-headed, metal-boned, swallowed it,
and so, by trickery, the moon was born:
Thoth, on a lotus flower, the blue baboon!

He crosses the celestial ocean
as helmsman of the world,
called Aah, the vizier of Ra, the sun.
He loads the gleaming boat
with palm leaves which record
the days and nights in notches,
for he is the measurer of time,
and he invented writing.
He carries an ivory writing palette
in his long black fingers, to instruct
the scribes who squat before him on the sand.

And he helps them on their later journey
through the Night Of A Million Years
as Thoth, the protector of the dead:
he takes them kindly by the hand
and guides them through the underworld;
his nine baboon musicians line
the long bank where the travellers
pass on their way to Osiris,
dreaming of playing draughts

with the gods and dancing with them
in the Field Of Reeds.

Mr Bonnet, did you meet him, and will I,
when I step on board the silver barque?
Will he be saying *Pleased to meet you,
Mrs Hill, and how's the writing going*?
as we descend the corridors of night
into the Judgment Hall. Will he pat me
on the shoulder with his cracked
avuncular hand and, tucking my book
inside his sky-blue cape, will he wink
before he picks his tail up and climbs
onto his special perch above the scales?

Below Hekla

I appear like a bird from nowhere.
I have a new name.
I am as clean as a whistle.
I beat the buttermilk in big white bowls
until it is smooth.
I wash the pearly plates under the tap,
and fifty canvas bumpers and fifty socks.
They drip in the sun
below grey mountains like the moon's.

Each night I lift the children
in their sleep and hold out
the china pot for them:
Wilt þú pissa, elskan,
pissa, pissa I whisper
as I tiptoe from bed to bed . . .
Around mid-night,
I go to the geyser below Hekla
and bathe in the warm water.

I am a short fat English girl.
I am twenty-five mothers.
I lead my children in a line
across the heather to the church.
The father watches me
from his dark door.
He shakes his head,
and takes me by the hand:
Blessa þú, elskan, blessa þú!

And now, September,
dust is flying: the bus is here.
I am ready.
I am on my way to Reykjavik,

Leith, Liverpool . . .
The children of the Barnaheimilið
are running to the gate like hens.
Good-bye, blessa þú,
give our love to the Beatles, good-bye.

The Fowlers of the Marshes

Three thousand years ago
they were fowling in the marshes
around Thebes – men in knotted skirts
and tiered faience collars,
who avoided the brown crocodile,
and loved the ibis, which they stalked
with long striped cats on strings,
under the eye of Nut, the goddess of the sky.

My mother's hushed peculiar world's the same:
she haunts it like the fowlers of the marshes,
tiptoeing gaily into history, sustained by gods
as strange to me as Lady Nut, and Anubis,
the oracular, the jackal-masked.
When I meet her at the station, I say
Hello, Mum! and think *Hello, Thoth,*
This is the Weighing of the Heart.

With Flaubert in the Koseir Desert

Do you remember the sherberts at Tortoni's?
You dip the spoon into the frosted glass,
you crush the little mound and lift the splinters
gently to your lips, you swoon with snowy joy.
Between you and me, Maxime, there's a shortage
of lemon ice in the wide Koseir desert!

I know Gustave. Nothing will stop him now.
Lemon ice! Lemon ice! he cries. Shut up, you fool,
My God, I'll kill you. But our good camels
break into a gallop – O Bir Ambar, the caravanserai!
We fill the calabash and drink and kiss,
ice-cold water dribbling from our chins.

Flaubert Writes a Letter Home

Flaubert, lying on Ibrahim's boat
in the middle of the Nile, is writing
to his mother. She wants him to think about
'une petite place', a little job, when he returns.
This makes him very cross –
She doesn't understand. 'All this ancient dust
makes one indifferent to fame' –
the sun, the sails, the Nile's quiet lapping.

A fellahin brings him dates and oranges.
All afternoon the Nubian sailors play
their darabukehs like a lullaby. He dreams
of Safia, 'his little Sophie', dancing
the Bee with Bambah for him in Esna,
their night together in the whitewashed room,
the rolls of her cunt unfolding like velvet,
and the bed-bugs that smelled of sandalwood.

'My dear old darling, if I get a position,
where would I be? Would I be more yours?
Think of that, my darling . . .'
This ploy of Flaubert's works.
She never mentions 'une petite place' again.
She wants him beside her at Croisset,
watching for early primulas under the lindens,
fishing for caluyots by moonlight.

Above Tooey Mountain

In comes Sister Payne, the midwife,
armed with newspaper, long gloves,
and a pudding-basin for the after-birth.
'Lie down and think of England',
says the Sister through her paper mask,
and the student nurse laughs
as she ties back her auburn hair.

You are born 'like greased lightning'
into the cold hands of the doctor.
He puts away the pethidine and kisses me.
'A beautiful boy!' he exclaims –
glad it's Friday, glad to be going away
on his long fishing week-end.

*

The Queen of Scots is this day
leichter of a fair son.
Brightness falls from the air,
from the hair, from the Queen's
son and heir. All this
the teachers taught us
before we were mothers.

*

There are people coming up the stairs
with flowers, to see
how sweet you are.
I smooth down my wavy hair
and tuck your shawl
behind your crumpled ear.

*

You cry so much
I stop visiting my mother.
You drive us all mad.
'Try giving him cooled camomile
or gripe-water,' she says.

*

*The child was not named
for two years, being called
simply wa-wa;
then there was a hair-cutting party,
and the child was given a llama.*

*

You stand in my bedroom
and watch me dress.
I kneel down so you can reach
the seven small buttons
that run down my back:

*

It is twilight in the park
behind the palace of the Archbishop.
The white football spins
between the groups of shivering boys.
'Wake up, Defence!
Do you want your face kicked in?'
A yellow dog cocks his leg
against the Memorial To The London Regiment.
*Remember The Fallen.
France And Flanders.
Salonika And Palestine.*
Are they all dead? And did it hurt?
You imagine soldiers' blood
trickling down Europe's
ice-cream-coloured map
like syrup.

*

You watch the ravens circle
above Tooey Mountain.
They can fly upside-down
and count to eight.
The largest passerine,
they pair for life. Their call
is a melancholy croak.

*

My Dear Jim, I cannot grasp
the great thoughts which are yours
much as I desire to do so.
Do not wear your soul out with tears
but be as usually brave.
If you get the little stove
be very careful with it.

*

I must get some sleep.
You won't be home tonight.
Born upstairs one Friday
in a room full of daffodils
and green lilies,
you have drifted away
to a tower of dreams
with only a dream-hole for light.

*

My Dearest Mother,
I am grieved that you should be
in such anxiety about me . . .
I am now in careful hands . . .
I have been in a sort of extremity of mind,
now I am the placidest soul in the world, Gerard.

*

The nurses hurry down
the darkened corridors
like rabbits, trying to be quiet,
like I was when I ran,
breathless from netball,
into the hushed chapel
for Hymn Practice:
'In the beauty of the lilies,
* Christ was borne across the sea,*
With a glory in his Bosom
* That transfigures you and me . . .'*
I sang too loudly, but my voice
was full of love.
Christ was my redeemer,
being born on a lily-pad.
I was Mary, his divine mother.

*

'Your son is ready. This way, please . . .'
I have been waiting to see you
all morning. The tall Sister
bends down to smooth your hair,
then takes away the tulips
I have brought for you –
my arms are damp
from holding them so long.

Dewpond and Black Drain-pipes

In order to distract me, my mother
sent me on an Archaeology Week.
We lived in tents on the downs,
and walked over to the site
every morning. It was an old dewpond.

There was a boy there called Charlie.
He was the first boy I had really met.
I was too shy to go to the pub,
but I hung around the camp every night
waiting for him to come back.

He took no notice of me at first,
but one night the two of us
were on Washing-Up together.
I was dressed in a black jersey
and black drain-pipes, I remember.

You in mourning? he said.
He didn't know I was
one of the first beatniks.
He put a drying-up cloth
over my head and kissed me

through the linen Breeds Of Dogs.
I love you, Charlie I said.
Later, my mother blamed herself
for what had happened. *The Romans
didn't even interest her*, she said.

Private View

I am the wife of the man who won first prize.
I am not wearing my new shoes which, though smarter,
are not so comfortable as these. I must stand well.
He's a very sensitive guy.
I'd really like to meet him.
Yes, he's obviously been through a lot.

Shoals of visitors move in and out of the exhibits.
My daughter won't shake hands.
Because the paint is spread so thick
the paintings look like toast.

Outside in the garden,
a foxglove leans against the trunk
of a tall sanded plane tree.
The evening sky is pale and magnificent.

Someone comes out onto the steps
and calls back *I'm going.*
He plunges into the cool air like a diver.
Shaking his yellow hair, he sees me
and smiles. He doesn't know
I am the wife of the man who won first prize.

Joy

It's him again,
the bird-man,
spinning round the corner
on his silver seven-speed bicycle –
looking so tall and pre-war
in his late father's flying helmet
and his long brown coat, like wings.

He opens the door of the studio
like some one whispering
Are you there? It's me,
holding a bunch of pink blossom
from the cherry tree.

He takes a plate of pastels
on his lap and rolls them
in a bed of powdered rice . . .
Gentlee gentlee catchee monkee . . .
5 cups of tea, and bright colours.
He's drawing in the blue.

Next time,
he brings his model with him.
Trip, trap, trip, up the stairs
go her tiny itchy feet.
So – she's flying out to Abu Simbel
at the week-end – a born traveller!
He swishes round her breast
with a stick of Burnt Siena
for the umpteenth time.
She looks like a Basking Shark.
Did you wash your face this morning?
he asks her as she goes –
Aah, cold cream . . . Everlasting Youth . . !

On Sunday, he paints the cherry tree.
He uses his brush like a toothpick
and the petals come lovely and clean.
Not a girl to be seen.
Sufficient unto the day,
as his mother used to say,
is the joy thereof.

He sits alone on his bed,
wrapped in the silk
peach-coloured happi-coat
his mother used to wear.
It's a hot summer night.
Thousands flock to beaches
to seek relief . . . I'm hot!
says topless redhead Miss Ramsgate.

He lets the Evening Standard
and The Layman's Tao Of Sex
slide to the floor — like a bather
who drops his towel on the beach
before swimming out to the rocks.
What silence! He's lost
in the curtains' orange pyramids,
and he's soon fast asleep,
packed like a mummy in cold cream . . .

His mother brushes his cheek
with the long red hair
she was so proud of,
and he covers her lips
with Violet . . .

As he wakes up,
he turns the radio on,
and says good-bye to his mother.

All the time, he whimpers,
I'm trying to think of a way
of getting out of this.
A voice like hers announces
a new travel deal for cyclists —
It's easier than you think, she says,
to be an Aeroflot cyclist.

Meanwhile, far away in Abu Simbel,
a young Egyptian prince
sits on a bed of camel-hair
and hammered gold and squeezes
a debutante from England,
like a boil, on his knee . . .
He's tormented by sand
and the girl's tight dress . . .
He's getting red in the face . . .
the hot tent . . . the joy thereof . . .
I am flying, Egypt, flying . . .

Inshallah – God Willing

Howard Carter went to Cairo
to send his telegram:
DISCOVERY COLOSSAL
NEED EVERY ASSISTANCE
and to order 32 bales of calico,
2 miles of surgical bandaging,
and 2000 yards of wadding.

Pecky Callender stayed
in the Valley of the Kings,
in the glare of the sun,
guarding the cutting
that led down to the treasure
with a loaded rifle
heavy on his knee.

And there was something else
on your mind, P.C.:
you had entered the chambers
already, on the night
of the 26th, breathing
illicitly that sweet air,
three millennia old –

sealed as long before Caesar
as Caesar is before us.
O Pecky Callender,
squatting on the edge of the desert
with beads of perspiration
on your fat head,
you have disturbed

the King's long night,
his holy body, gravely anointed
and sweetly-smelling,
his proud eyes
'that long behold felicity',
and the flowers
still fresh in the tomb;

you have disturbed
black Anubis, the jackal,
and the blue-eyed cheetah,
the golden sentinels,
the four bare-footed
goddesses of the underworld,
and the god of eternity, Heh.

Abdul Ali, your servant,
when he saw the yellow canary
you bought from the market
at Karnak, cried out
Inshallah – god willing –
it's a bird of gold, Mabrook,
it'll bring good luck in the valley!

After the gold was discovered,
and you came back late
to the rest house, over the sound
of your donkey padding on the sand,
you heard someone call
for a light, and the door
of your room stood open.

Elegy for the Bee-god

Stingless bees
were bred in tree hollows
for beeswax and honey.
Every year, in the month
called Tzec, the bee-keepers
played their raspadores
and danced across the fields
with bells and ribbons
round their feet, to honour
the fat bee-god, who buzzed
in the heated air
to their music.
He lived in a gold house
in the hotlands, and drank
cocoa sweetened with honey.

All's quiet now, it's June,
and he's not here, the late,
the long-forgotten bee-god,
who sped on zig-zag wings
across the sky to the faithful.
Cross-eyed, bejewelled
and tattooed, drumming
his fluffy yellow feet
on the tree hollows,
he gave the bees new hope,
and cocoa sweetened with honey.

If ever I find him – thin,
justly offended, dead
in the dry chaparral –
I will put jade beads
and honey on his tongue,
and wrap him in a shroud

of wings, and loop his neck
with pearls from Guatemala;
I will light him candles
of beeswax, bringing sleep,
and he will rest in the shade
of the First Tree,
and wait for me there —
humming a tune, and drinking
cocoa sweetened with honey.

A Voice in the Garden

Gerald's here! my mother called,
Are you ready? The taxi was waiting
to take us to our weekly swimming lessons.
I drove through Marylebone like a V.I.P.
our kind neighbour close beside me,
smelling of soap and peppermint . . .
He squatted on the edge of the pool
and shouted *One, two! One, two!* as I struggled
with the water like a kitten. I kept my eyes
on the gold buttons of his blazer.
They were as smooth and glossy
as the boiled sweets he liked to suck,
and offer to his young friends.
I sank and kicked and spat out water.
The bright buttons rose and fell . . .

And then one day he came in beside me,
his old grey body quaking
like a mollusc without its shell.
The wet wool of his bathing trunks
reminded me of blankets I had peed on.
His hands in the moving water
seemed to float between my legs.
He smiled. I swam to the edge of the pool
and pulled myself over the steps.
The heated water trickled down my legs
as I wrapped my towel round me, like a shawl.
That was our last swimming lesson,
but he still came to tea on Sundays,
after his 'little siesta',
and sat down in the seat next to mine.

As he listened to my mother –
picking his biscuits off his plate
with pink eager fingers, lifting
his tea-cup to his lips, and nodding –
he pressed a silver florin in my hand.
I kept them in a muff in my drawer,
under my uniform. At last I poured them
into a plastic bag and took them by bus
to The Little Sisters Of The Poor
in Albert Street . . . Next Sunday, I hid
in the garden, but he came pushing his way
through the roses, looking for me.
I heard the twigs breaking up, and his voice
in the bushes calling and calling –
Yoo-hoo, Gerald's here, yoo-hoo . . .

The Letter-writer

There has been no letter for two weeks.
Someone must have seen you –
as they opened their shop in the morning
or, loosening their hair by the window,
they may have seen you cross the fields
and thought *He's out late,* and little more.
For me, you being there's as strange
as a man in a tiny aeroplane,

who pours his milk, drinks his tea,
twenty-five thousand feet up
like a picnicker in the sky.
From the ground, there is only a dot
visible, and the trail of white smoke,
that crosses the sky, diminishes,
then disappears altogether
beyond the rim of the clouds.

The Ram

He jangles his keys in the rain
and I follow like a lamb.
His house is as smoky as a dive.
We go straight downstairs to his room.

I lie on his bed and watch him
undress. His orange baseball jacket,
all the way from Ontario,
drops to the floor – THE RAMS, in felt,

arched across the hunky back.
He unzips his calf-length
Star-walkers, his damp black Levi's,
and adjusts his loaded modelling-pouch:

he stands before me in his socks –
as white as bridesmaids,
little daisies, driven snow.
John Wain watches from the wall

beside a shelf-ful of pistols.
Well, he says, *d'you like it?*
All I can think of is Granny,
how she used to shake her head,

when I stood by her bed on Sundays,
so proud in my soap-smelling
special frock, and say *Ah,*
Bless your little cotton socks!

The Diving Archaeologists

Led to the Sacred Well of Sacrifice
by the ancient peculiar map
of Diego de Landa, the archbishop,
here in the hot jungle,
where temples sink in mud,
he decides to send for Paterson,
the diver, who is gathering sponges
off the Bahama Islands.

Bound virgins, carrying jade
and chipped obsidian to appease
the glittering serpents,
were thrown into the well
by singing priests at daybreak —
fair female appellants
sent to talk to the goddess
and reason with her under water.

The divers, weighted by their new
iron shoes and necklaces of lead,
are let down into the well
by native boys, who are crying.
The air-valves go pht! pht!
as the waters close
and the light rays
change to purple.

Sunk on ledges, in soft
gruel-thick mud, they find
drowned women's bones, and nodules
of yellow perfumed resin,
and the presents of jade
and obsidian, carefully

broken by the priests
to release their sacred spirits.

When the divers surface,
trailing slimy loops of weed
like hair, their helmets
bump against the bottom of the raft.
The native boys throw down
their wide bleached hats
in fear, and call out
on the swaying pontoon:

El Amo! The Master!
In her anger, the goddess
has swallowed him,
and now she comes knocking,
as a warning — we must not
go down where the women hold
their secret meetings,
in the Well of Chichén Itzá.

The Goose

Rhamia, their only child, is coming home!
Not since the day they kissed her
and she drove away to be a muslim
has there been such life at the Vicarage.
They hurry down to the orchard to call Boo,
the goose. She runs up like a lamb
and pokes her white neck into their basket —
on the look-out for food as usual.
In the kitchen Cook is podding bowls of peas
in front of an open recipe book.
Garnish with watercress. Stuff with sage.
She chops up the onions and feels tears
run down her cheeks like mercury.

                    *

Rhamia, who used to be called Jenny,
walks out of the drawing-room.
She calls to Abdullah, her son,
Come out to the yard now, and the boy
comes running. His old grand-parents
watch him from the window.
He slits the white neck of the goose
with a carving-knife and as the blood
runs over his wrists he calls out
Allah! Allah! His high child's voice
rings out across the fields.
Then he takes the body in to Cook,
who is rolling out pastry in the kitchen.

The Picnic
for Rose

I

We used to shave our armpits
as smooth as a baby's bottom.
She always left hers hairy.
How we admired her!

She ran away to Wales
and became a farmer's wife,
and a Methodist. She kept goats
on the hill behind the chapel.

Then she joined the ashram
at Poona, leaving her sons
in Paris. She worked in the laundry
and stopped writing home.

And now she's alone
on the north coast of Norfolk,
considering Russian Orthodoxy
beside an icy sea.

II

Consider the Ancient Egyptians,
the most religious of all!
Their gods are very hospitable,
and like to travel around.
The broads and salt marshes
might suit them.
They could come soon,
in their sacred barges,
made from cedarwood
of Lebanon, all gilded.

Build them sanctuaries
at Sheringham on the sand.
Call Min, the thunderbolt,
from Coptos, and his priest
the chemist, who concocts
'the divine substance'
in his long glass tubes,
and the bee-keeping priests
who make honey, because Min
is very fond of honey.

Open the door of his shrine
and give him some grain
for the morning. Dress him
in his plumed head-dress
and bring him from the chill
holy-of-holies into the light.
We will worship him, the tall
ithyphallic lover-lover,
we will lift up our skirts
and get drunk . . .

III

Let's all go for a picnic.
We will pack baskets
of rolls and lemonade
and make our way

over the white dunes
to the shore. We will spread
striped towels
along the shingle beach

and watch the gods, happy
in their swimming-trunks,

collecting shells,
and doing press-ups on the sand,

and the tall priests,
knee-deep in turquoise,
splashing their shoulders
with water, and shouting;

then, rolling over
on the stones, we'll lie
like seals in the sun,
letting their voices wash over us.

The Flowers

After lunch my daughter picked
handfuls of the wild flowers
she knew her grandfather liked best
and piled them in the basket of her bicycle,
beside an empty jam-jar and a trowel;
then, swaying like a candle-bearer,
she rode off to the church
and, like a little dog, I followed her.

She cleared the grave of nettles
and wild parsley, and dug a shallow hole
to put the jam-jar in. She arranged
the flowers to look their best
and scraped the moss from the stone,
so you could see whose grave
she had been caring for.
It didn't take her long – no longer
than making his bed in the morning
when he had got too old to help her.

Not knowing how to leave him,
how to say good-bye, I hesitated
by the rounded grave. *Come on,*
my daughter said, *It's finished now.*
And so we got our bicycles and rode home
down the lane, moving apart
and coming together again,
in and out of the ruts.

The Bicycle Ride

I step into the Autumn morning
like a First Communicant
and ride off down the lane,
singing.
Across the frosty fields
someone is mending fences
knock knock knock,
and a twig that's caught
in my bicycle spokes
tinkles like a musical box.
The village smells of wood-ash
and warm horses.
Shining crows rise
into the sky like hymns.

I have to pass the church
where my father was buried.
It's a wonderful church.
The Christ in the chancel
is carved by Eric Gill.
There are guidebooks in the nave,
and every day the villagers come
to put fresh flowers
on the graves. My father's
is under the yew tree
by the wall. I look at it
out of the corner of my eye
as I go cycling past,
making for open country.

We didn't go this way
after the funeral –
my mother and me,

and my sad unfamiliar aunts
crying and crying
for their lost brother.
In hired cars,
we went straight home,
where some kind person
had made us tea
and tiny sandwiches.
They were like pocket-handkerchiefs.
Pat, pat, pat . . . My father
used to dry my tears like that.

Down by the Salley Gardens

You are stamping squares of turf down
with your boots, where you have planted bulbs.
At the open window someone is playing
'Down By The Salley Gardens'
on an old piano, and singing.
You straighten up from time to time
and rub the small of your back.

One of your children puts a wedding album
open on the table, and runs away laughing.
Here you are on tiptoe, winding
flowers in your hair. Your new husband
leads you towards a lawn-ful of ladies
under a shower of confetti. Darling,
you are their bride! How they love you!

A hundred ghosts are watching you
as you come up to the back door
with your bag of bulbs.
You push some hair under your scarf
with hands as muddy as paws.
Don't listen to the sad music —
'the weirs . . . the little snow-white feet . . .'

Ty-Coch

And now the snow has fallen
over the house where we were lovers
and the weight of the snow
has made the roof cave in.

They have taken away the timbers,
and put the bed out on the terrace
where the roses used to grow.
Snow surrounds the house

in drifts, like bears;
and sheep, come down off the mountain,
shelter in the room
we used to love in.

Among the Thyme and Daisies

We climbed in bare feet to the barrow –
losing the path, tumbling
over rabbit-holes, turning round
from time to time to see
how small the villages were getting.

We reached the first chalk foot
exhausted. The sky seemed nearer,
friendlier, baby-blue. We walked along
the giant's flowery legs, tickling
his fat thighs like ants.

When we found the head,
we closed our eyes and wished –
for something new and wonderful;
we never thought of the Future,
or wished for that.

And now, approaching forty,
I feel like a giantess myself –
vain, drowsy, out-of-date,
ruminating on my hill
among the thyme and daisies.

I hear the children holler
down the rabbit-burrows,
and feel them climbing my legs;
there is grass growing over my face,
and a wonderful view of the sky.

Chicken Feathers

I

What a picture!
She has tucked her wild-looking chicken
under her arm and stares out
over what seems to be a mountain pass
on a windy day.
She is wearing a blue linen dress
the colour of summer.
She reminds me of Brunhilde –
alone, bronzed, unfamiliar.
She doesn't look like anybody's mother.

II

She used to love dancing.
She went to the Chelsea Ball
dressed as a leopard;
there she met my father,
who looked so dashing
in the Harlequin suit
his tailor made for him
from raw silk.
He had tiny shoes
like Cinderella's.
I have seen them.

III

She comes to collect me from school,
on time, silent,
and I hand her my coat and satchel –
avoiding, even then, her lovely eyes,
that look down on my world
like distant stars.
I play with the girl next door,
and don't come home till bed-time.

IV

From the lighted window
I watch my mother
picking leeks in the twilight.

I will have soup
for my supper,
sprinkled with parsley.

She passes me my creamy bowl.
My hands are warm,
and smell of soap.

My mother's hands are cold as roots.
She shuts up the chickens
by moonlight.

V

How can they think I am asleep
when he bends down and kisses
the nape of her neck,
and goes away to his own room,
while she sits in front of her mirror
and brushes and brushes
her waist-long silver hair?

VI

The hens are all gone.
How happy she used to be
setting out in her long tweed coat
across the orchard
with her bucket.
Chuck, chuck, chuck, she called
and they'd all come running.

VII

She walks behind the hedges
of the large garden, stooping
from time to time

to pick narcissi
for her mother's grave,
now that it is Easter.
We don't want to go.
We're too young to remember
our grandmother —
and besides it will be cold
in the grave-yard
where the wind blows
straight in off the downs.

VIII

He went to his room with an orange
in his hand, and died there
sometime during the afternoon.
My mother spent the day in the kitchen.
When I came in from the garden
I was sent upstairs
to call him down to tea:
He was sitting by the window
with his back to me.
On the table beside him
were four boats made of orange peel,
with the pith piled neatly inside them.
My mother couldn't stand up.
She kept on saying she was sorry,
but she couldn't stand up.
It must be the shock she said.
It wasn't grief.
Come and sit down she said,
And have your tea.

IX

Tonight I kissed my mother,
for the first time that I can remember;
though I must have kissed her before,
as all daughters kiss their mothers.

She was passing in front of me
to kiss the children, and I leant down
and touched her cheek with my lips.
It was easy — like the lighting of a candle.

X

My sister always says
that on the morning our father died
he was working on a drawing of a liner
disappearing over a white horizon.
She says it is a symbol.
She's got the picture by her bed.
I would rather think of dying
as a coming into harbour,
a sort of final mooring.

XI

You put in at a little jetty.
There is someone there to welcome you —
not sinister — but rather surprising —
someone you know. In front of you rise
banks of fern and shining celandines.
You can smell the woods.
They are full of life,
but very still.

XII

My mother and I, in our way,
understand each other.
When I kneel by her grave,
in need of a little consolation,
I will picture her standing
on a hillside in bright sunlight,
lifting her hand to wave to me;
or is she brushing away the feathers
that drift like dreams into her hair
and tickle her cheek, till she smiles.

SAYING HELLO
AT THE STATION